Flowerscape

A BOTANICAL COLORING BOOK

BY MAGGIE ENTERRIOS

PAGE STREET
PUBLISHING CO.

PAGE STREET
PUBLISHING CO.

First published in 2021 by
Page Street Publishing Co.
27 Congress Street, Suite 1511
Salem, MA 01970
www.pagestreetpublishing.com

Distributed by Macmillan, sales in Canada by The Canadian Manda Group.

25   24   23   22   5

ISBN-13: 978-1-64567-216-6
ISBN-10: 1-64567-216-6

Illustrations by Maggie Enterrios
Cover design by Maggie Enterrios
Cover lettering by Adé Hogue

Printed and bound in China

THIS BOOK BELONGS TO

WELCOME TO FLOWERSCAPE

INTRODUCTION

Flowerscape is your escape to a world that is bursting with abundant blooms, twirling vines and hidden creatures. Imagine yourself wandering through a flourishing garden: Relax, reframe and allow yourself to freely thrive in creativity. Watch the pages spring to life with every step as you play through these lush illustrations and geometric designs.

There is no right way to fill these pages. Whether you choose to color, to shade or to doodle additional plants and animals, let your creativity lead the way. I have built a foundation of botanical illustrations that await your contribution. In adding your unique touch to each page, you are truly finishing the story that I began, creating a gorgeous, collaborative work of art. Share your coloring online by tagging @ColorFlowerscape and #Flowerscape.

No matter where you are, let *Flowerscape* take you to a place filled with beauty and growth. There are no thorns in this garden—only joy.

CLEMATIS

DECORATIVE DAHLIA

BALL DAHLIA

TWINFLOWER

DAFFODIL

TRUMPET FLOWER

GOLDEN WATTLE

BIRD OF PARADISE

MONSTERA

MORNING BEAUTY ECHEVERIA

STARGAZER LILY

COLUMBINE

CROCOSMIA

CHRYSANTHEMUM

LILY OF THE VALLEY

ASTER

PLUMBAGO

FOXGLOVE

HIBISCUS

TREASURE FLOWER

IXORA

ENGLISH ROSE

LUPINE

MARIGOLD

ORCHID

PEONY

PORCELAIN FLOWERS

PROTEA

PANSY

VIOLA

SPIDER PLANT

APRICOT BLOSSOM

TRILLIUM

HYACINTH

HYBRID TEA ROSE

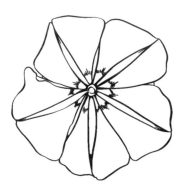

MORNING GLORY

FREESIA

COSMOS

FRANGIPANI

DAPHNE

ZINNIA

FUCHSIA

ABOUT THE ARTIST

MAGGIE ENTERRIOS draws pretty things and has been doing so professionally since 2010. As a commercial illustrator, published author and speaker, Maggie is most known for her dense style of botanical illustration and pattern creation. Maggie considers herself a maximalist and thrives in the intricate details of design, drawing inspiration from the ornamental styles of the Art Nouveau and Arts & Crafts movements. After attending art school and starting her creative career in Chicago, Maggie now spends much of her time traveling: chasing summertime and delighting in nature in bloom.

Flowerscape is Maggie's third publication and her first coloring book. Previously, she created *Nature Observer: A Guided Journal* (2017) and *Gather: A Foraging Journal* (2018). More of her work can be found at www.littlepatterns.com or on social media @littlepatterns.

When she is not creating art, Maggie spends her time cooking ambitious meals, preferably dirtying every pot along the way.